GOOD PEOPLE BEHAVING BADLY

CAUTIONARY TALES TO HELP US AVOID COSTLY MISTAKES

CREATED BY TIERCE GREEN

GOOD FEED
MEDIA

GOOD PEOPLE BEHAVING BADLY

Published by **Good Feed Media**

Copyright 2025 Tierce Green Ministries, Inc.

All rights reserved.

ISBN: 979-8-9921538-2-8

This book supports the video content created and presented by Tierce Green. There are eight sessions in the series. Each session is about 25 minutes.

Video sessions for this series are completely FREE within the Good Feed Media App. There is no obligation to pay anything, but you have the opportunity to help us KEEP IT FREE by paying it forward.

Order additional copies of this resource and high-definition videos of this series for public viewing from Good Feed Media.

GOOD FEED
MEDIA
FREE APP. FREE CONTENT.

ORDER RESOURCES AND DOWNLOAD THE APP AT GOODFEEDMEDIA.COM

Good Feed Media is a division of Tierce Green Ministries, Inc.

Video production by Layne Laughter.

Cover photo by Karim Elgamil on Unsplash.

Distributed by:

Tierce Green Ministries, Inc.

The Woodlands, TX

tiercegreen.com

CONTENTS

ABOUT THE CONTENT

A cautionary tale is a story that serves as a warning to others. Fairy tales contain cautionary elements. Pinocchio warns against lying, and Little Red Riding Hood teaches children to be careful when encountering strangers. Our daily news feeds deliver an endless stream of cautionary tales, stories covering everything from economic mismanagement to exposés about moral decline and failure.

Here's our dilemma: Humans are slow learners, and adjusting our course to steer clear of danger is challenging. No matter how devastating the outcome of previous bad choices, we tend to be repeat offenders. We ignore the warning signs and build our houses closer and closer to the cliff.

The Bible is packed with stories that capture men and women at their best and worst. It contains true-story cautionary tales that place God's presence, power, and grace in the midst of it all. No one intentionally auditions for a starring role in a cautionary tale. We typically stumble into it or stubbornly walk down a path while ignoring the warning signs.

In these eight sessions, we'll look at a collection of cautionary tales to help us avoid making the same costly mistakes. Watching the sessions alone is a less-than experience. The best experience is to go through this series with others and process the principles together. You need the encouragement and perspective of others. And others need the same from you.

Video sessions of this content can be freely accessed on the Good Feed Media App. Learn more and download at GOODFEEDMEDIA.COM

ABOUT THE AUTHOR

Tierce Green has over 45 years of professional ministry experience, including 30 years as a full-time speaker for conferences and retreats and 15 years of local church ministry. He served as a Student Pastor in a church of 1,200 and an Executive Pastor in a church of 12,000, where he led over a thousand men each week for seven years in a seasonal gathering called The Quest.

Tierce is on the presentation team of 33 The Series for Authentic Manhood, which has reached over three million men worldwide. He is the Director of Authentic Manhood Initiative, coaching leaders to reach men with the principles of biblical manhood. He is also the Director of **Good Feed Media**, creating quality disciple-making content freely available on the Good Feed Media App.

Tierce and his wife, Dana, have one daughter, Anna, and live in The Woodlands, TX.

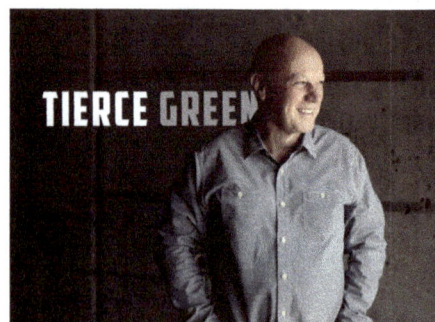

1

GRAPES, GIANTS, GRASSHOPPERS, AND GOD

I. CAUTIONARY TALES

A. Humans are slow learners.

   1. Most people don't intentionally audition for a starring role in a cautionary tale.

   2. We typically stumble into it or stubbornly walk down a path while ignoring the warning signs.

B. The Bible is packed with true-story cautionary tales.

   1. It captures men and women at their best and worst.

   2. It places God's presence, power, and grace in the midst of it all.

II. THE BAD BEHAVIOR OF A NATION

A. Why is it important?

   1. Examples for us.

   • 1 Corinthians 10:1-6 // For I do not want you to be ignorant of the fact, brothers and sisters, that our ancestors were all under the cloud and that they all passed through the sea … They all ate the same spiritual food and drank the same spiritual drink. For they drank from the spiritual rock that accompanied them, and that rock was Christ. Nevertheless, God was not pleased with most of them. Their bodies were scattered in the wilderness. Now these things occurred as **examples** to keep us from setting our hearts on evil things as they did. (NIV)

2. Warnings for us.

- 1 Corinthians 10:11-12 // These things happened to them as examples and were written down as **warnings** for us … So, if you think you are standing firm, be careful that you don't fall! (NIV)

III. GOD'S PURPOSE, PRESENCE, GUIDANCE, AND PROVISION

A. The Israelites were enslaved and oppressed by the Egyptians. (Exodus 1)

B. The call of Moses. (Exodus 3)

C. The confrontation with Pharaoh.

- Exodus 5:1 // Moses and Aaron went to Pharaoh and said, "This is what the Lord, the God of Israel, says: 'Let my people go, so that they may hold a festival to me in the wilderness.'" (NIV)

D. Ten plagues devastated the land of Egypt and its people. (Exodus 7-12)

- The Nile River and all the water turned to blood, frogs, lice, flies, livestock pestilence, boils, hail, darkness, and the killing of the firstborn.

E. The mass exodus from Egypt.

- This was one of the largest migrations in the history of the world.

- Exodus 12 records about 600,000 men on foot, plus women and children, bringing the total number of Israelites to about two million. It mentions many other people who also left with them and large droves of livestock. The logistics were massive and nothing short of miraculous.

F. God made it clear that in doing this for His people, He would also reveal Himself to the Egyptians.

- Exodus 7:5 // And the Egyptians will know that I am the Lord when I stretch out my hand against Egypt and bring the Israelites out of it. (NIV)

Whatever God is doing in us or for us, there is always a bigger purpose of what He can do through us to reveal Himself to the world.

- When we get in sync with God's bigger purpose, we begin to experience the full and meaningful life He created us to live.

G. God's purpose, presence, guidance, and provision for His people were evident every step of the way.

- Exodus 13:21-22 // By day, the Lord went ahead of them in a pillar of cloud to guide them on their way and by night in a pillar of fire to give them light so that they could travel by day or night. Neither the pillar of cloud by day nor the pillar of fire by night left its place in front of the people. (NIV)

IV. CHRONIC BAD BEHAVIOR

A. Showdown at the Red Sea.

-   The people panicked. (Exodus 14:10-12)

-   God provided. (Exodus 14:29-31)

B. Three days after the Red Sea miracle, the Israelites couldn't find water to drink.

-   Instead of trusting God, they grumbled and complained ... again. (Exodus 15:24)

V. RECON OF THE PROMISED LAND

A. A team was chosen to check out the land, the people, and the towns, and to bring back samples of the fruit.

-   Numbers 13:21-25 // So they went up and explored the land ... When they reached the Valley of Eshkol, they cut off a branch bearing a single cluster of grapes. Two of them carried it on a pole between them, along with some pomegranates and figs ... At the end of forty days they returned from exploring the land. (NIV)

B. The assessment.

-   Numbers 13:27-33 // They gave Moses this account: "We went into the land to which you sent us, and it does flow with milk and honey! Here is its fruit. But the people who live there are powerful, and the cities are fortified and very large. We even saw descendants of Anak there ..."

Then Caleb silenced the people before Moses and said, "We should go up and take possession of the land, for we can certainly do it."

But the men who had gone up with him said, "We can't attack those people. They are stronger than we are." And they spread among the Israelites a bad report about the land they had explored. They said, "The land we explored devours those living in it. All the people we saw there are of great size. We saw the Nephilim there [the giants] … We seemed like grasshoppers in our own eyes, and we looked the same to them." (NIV)

VI. GRAPES, GIANTS, GRASSHOPPERS, AND GOD

■ GRAPES = The Fruit of the Promised Life

- Galatians 5:22-23 // The fruit of the Spirit is love, joy, peace, patience, kindness, goodness, faithfulness, gentleness, self-control … (ESV)

- Philippians 2:12 // Continue to work out your salvation with fear and trembling … (NIV)

- John 7:38 // Whoever believes in me … "Out of his heart will flow rivers of living water." (NIV)

- John 15:5 // I am the vine, you are the branches. If you remain in me and I in you, you will bear much fruit … (NIV)

- John 10:10 // The thief comes only to steal and kill and destroy. I have come that they may have life, and have it to the full. (NIV)

■ GIANTS = The Enemies of the Promised Life

- Ephesians 6:12 // For our struggle is not against flesh and blood but against the rulers, against the authorities, against the powers of this dark world, and against the spiritual forces of evil in the heavenly realms. (NIV)

- Our biggest giants are CONTROL, COMFORT, and SIGNIFICANCE.

■ GRASSHOPPERS = People Who Rob Themselves of the Promised Life

- Numbers 13:32-33 // All the people we saw there are of great size. We saw the Nephilim [the giants] ... We seemed like grasshoppers in our own eyes, and we looked the same to them. (NIV)

- Ten of the twelve had a limited horizontal vision.

- Caleb and Joshua had the advantage of clear vertical vision.

■ GOD = A Display of His Righteousness, Mercy, and Justice

- Numbers 14:10-12 // Then, the glory of the Lord appeared at the tent of meeting to all the Israelites. The Lord said to Moses, "How long will these people treat me with contempt? How long will they refuse to believe in me In spite of all the signs I have performed among them? I will strike them down with a plague and destroy them, but I will make you into a nation greater and stronger than they." (NIV)

- Numbers 14:20-23 // The Lord replied, "I have forgiven them, as you asked. Nevertheless, as surely as I live and as surely as the glory of the Lord fills the whole earth, not one of those who saw my glory and the signs I performed in Egypt and in the wilderness but who disobeyed me and tested me ten times—not one of them will ever see the land I promised on oath to their ancestors. No one who has treated me with contempt will ever see it." (NIV)

VII. WHAT'S AT STAKE

A. The full and meaningful life God created us to live. (John 10:10)

B. Eternal rewards at the Judgement Seat of Christ.

- 2 Corinthians 5:10 // We must all appear before the Judgment Seat of Christ so that each of us may receive what is due us for the things done while in the body, whether good or bad. (NIV)

The Judgement Seat of Christ is not about judging our sins but about judging our works as followers of Jesus. Works have nothing to do with salvation because our foundation is Jesus. The rewards are based on how we have built on that foundation.

- 1 Corinthians 3:11-15 // For no one can lay any foundation other than the one already laid, which is Jesus Christ. If anyone builds on this foundation using gold, silver, costly stones, wood, hay, or straw, their work will be shown for what it is because the Day will bring it to light.

It will be revealed with fire, and the fire will test the quality of each person's work. If what has been built survives, the builder will receive a reward. If it is burned up, the builder will suffer loss but yet will be saved—even though only as one escaping through the flames. (NIV)

- 1 Corinthians 9:24-25 // Do you not know that in a race, all the runners run, but only one gets the prize? Run in such a way as to get the prize. Everyone who competes in the games goes into strict training. They do it to get a crown that will not last, but we do it to get a crown that will last forever. (NIV)

- Revelation 4:10-11 // The twenty-four elders fall down before him who sits on the throne and worship him who lives forever and ever. They lay their crowns before the throne and say: "You are worthy, our Lord and God, to receive glory and honor and power, for you created all things, and by your will they were created and have their being." (NIV)

C. Influence on future generations.

- Numbers 14:33 // Your children will be shepherds here for forty years, suffering for your unfaithfulness, until the last of your bodies lies in the wilderness. (NIV)

Children will leave with what their parents have lived out at home.

VIII. FINAL THOUGHTS

- How we respond to our imperfections determines the kind of legacy we leave. If we are humble and teachable, we will model for the next generation what it looks like to follow Jesus.

- The Fruit of the Promised Life is available to all because of God's amazing grace. No matter what your story has been, it doesn't have to end as a cautionary tale.

TALK ABOUT IT

1. How has God's guidance and provision in the past helped you trust Him with challenges in the present?

2. The Fruit of the Spirit is evidence of the presence of Jesus and the filling of the Holy Spirit. Look at the fruit list: love, joy, peace, patience, kindness, goodness, faithfulness, gentleness, self-control. Which ones are evident in your life? Which ones need cultivating?

3. God can use difficult circumstances to reveal our giants—the enemies of the promised life. Giants can be things like unforgiveness, bitterness, jealousy, pride, self-righteousness, anger, and laziness. How has God used circumstances to reveal your giants?

4. Grasshoppers are controlled by fear. How has God helped you face your fears?

5. Talk about the rewards at the Judgement Seat of Christ. Have you heard of this principle before? Does it inspire you or concern you? How can you use it as a positive motivator as you follow Jesus?

NOTES

NOTES

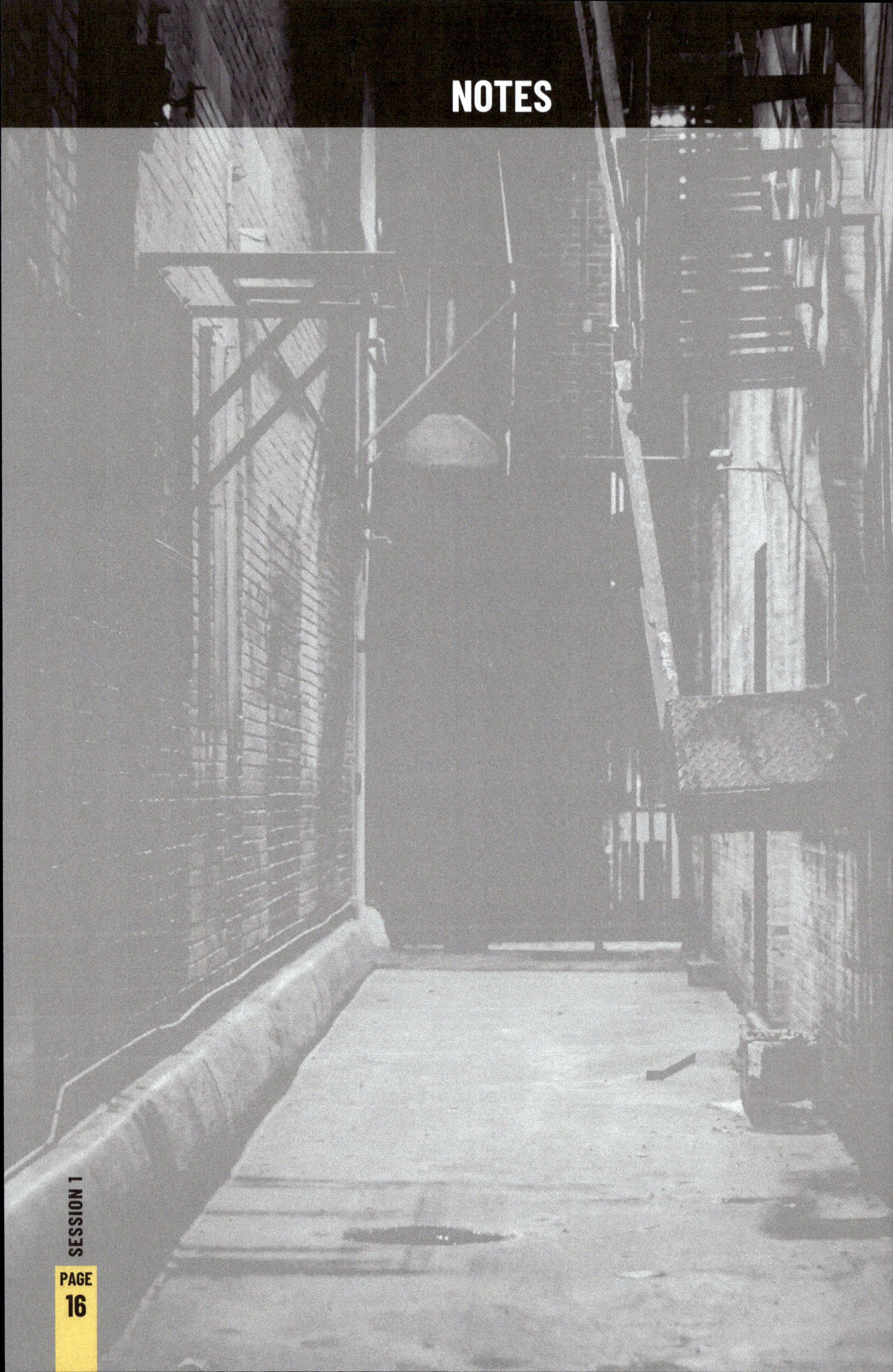

2

TALL, DARK, AND TORMENTED

GOOD
PEOPLE
BEHAVING
BADLY

I. INTRODUCTION

A. The tragic story of King Saul, Israel's first king.

- About 450 years have passed from the time we left "these grumbling Israelites," as God described them, in the wilderness.

B. Saul's story begins with Samuel.

- Samuel was Israel's last judge and first prophet.

- Samuel's success began as a boy, under his mentor Eli, a priest and judge of Israel. God called Samuel to replace Eli, whose sons were wicked.

- Samuel was a humble servant of Israel. His motivation was not power but service. People listened because they recognized his sincerity and genuine concern for their well-being.

- Samuel's integrity and character were not transferred to his sons. They accepted bribes and perverted justice.

- When Samuel grew old, he appointed his sons as Israel's leaders.

- The elders of Israel could see that Samuel's sons lacked his integrity and did not want to be led by them. God was their king, but they demanded a human king.

- God instructed Samuel to warn the people of everything they would lose under submission to the rights of a king. But they refused to listen, and so God told Samuel to give them what they wanted.

II. GOD'S WILL AND WHAT HE ALLOWS

KEY LESSON #1

A. God doesn't force us to comply with His will.

- God gives us the choice to work with Him or not.

- He wants our relationship with Him to be … relational—for us to love Him with all our heart, soul, mind, and strength—and to love working with Him.

KEY LESSON #2

B. Sometimes, God will give us what we want, even though it's not what we need.

- Whatever God allows is always for a bigger purpose and part of His divine plan.

- God may allow us to suffer so we can see what He sees—flaws in our character and flaws in our faith—for the purpose of healing us and strengthening us.[1]

C. Israel's demand for a king revealed a deeper problem.

- They were repeating the bad behavior of their ancestors.

- 1 Samuel 8:7-8 // And the Lord told him: "Listen to all that the people are saying

---

[1] Learn more about this principle in *Life Interrupted—Finding Peace in the Detours, Dead Ends, and Disappointments*, an 8-session series on Good Feed Media. Download the App at GOODFEEDMEDIA.COM

to you. It is not you they have rejected, but they have rejected me as their king. As they have done from the day I brought them up out of Egypt until this day, forsaking me and serving other gods, so they are doing to you." (NIV)

- 1 Corinthians 10:11 // These things happened to them as examples and were written down as warnings for us. (NIV)

III. TALL, DARK, AND HANDSOME

KEY LESSON #3

A. We have an unhealthy attraction to external appearances.

- 1 Samuel 9:2 // Kish had a son named Saul, as handsome a young man as could be found anywhere in Israel, and he was a head taller than anyone else.

- This was not the only time Saul's physical appearance was emphasized.

B. Saul is revealed as Israel's king.

- 1 Samuel 9:15-17 // Now, the day before Saul came, the Lord had revealed this to Samuel: "About this time tomorrow, I will send you a man from the land of Benjamin. Anoint him ruler over my people, Israel. He will deliver them from the hand of the Philistines. I have looked on my people, for their cry has reached me."

  When Samuel caught sight of Saul, the Lord said to him, "This is the man I spoke to you about. He will govern my people." (NIV)

KEY LESSON #4

C. Was it humility or insecurity?

- 1 Samuel 9:21 // Saul answered, "But am I not a Benjamite, from the smallest tribe of Israel, and is not my clan the least of all the clans of the tribe of Benjamin? Why do you say such a thing to me?" (NIV)

- Insecurity, if left unchecked, can lead to bad decisions driven by a craving for approval.

- Saul's insecurity eventually caused him to give in to paranoia and sink into depression.

D. The Spirit of the Lord came powerfully upon Saul. (1 Samuel 10)

- In the Old Testament, the Spirit of God would temporarily come upon people and empower them for a purpose.

- In the New Testament, since Pentecost, the Holy Spirit lives in us by God's grace and through our faith—a sign of a true believer.

- Romans 8:9 // If anyone does not have the Spirit of Christ, they do not belong to Christ. (NIV)

E. Saul was a passionate 30-year-old warrior king. (1 Samuel 11:6)

- Three hundred thousand men from Israel and thirty thousand men from Judah were united to rescue the people of Jabesh Gilead.

- Saul initially directed the attention to God. (1 Samuel 11:13)

IV. CHARACTER FLAWS

A. Fear-Driven Disobedience

- Saul's troops were quaking in fear of the Philistines and scattering. He was supposed to wait seven days for Samuel to arrive and make the burnt offering, but Samuel was late, and Saul was impatient.

- Saul assumed the role of priest and made the burnt offering.

- 1 Samuel 13:13 // "You have done a foolish thing," Samuel said. "You have not kept the command the Lord your God gave you. If you had, he would have established your kingdom over Israel for all time." (NIV)

B. Selective Obedience (1 Samuel 15)

- Selective Obedience is the same as disobedience.

- Selective Obedience says, "It's okay if I didn't do that because I did this!"

C. Pride and Arrogance

- When Samuel went looking for Saul, he was told that the king had gone to Carmel, where he had set up a monument in his own honor.

- 1 Samuel 15:13 // When Samuel reached him, Saul said, "The Lord bless you! I have carried out the Lord's instructions." (NIV)

- Samuel called him out:

1 Samuel 15:17-23 // Samuel said, "Although you were once small in your own eyes, did you not become the head of the tribes of Israel? The Lord anointed you king over Israel. And he sent you on a mission, saying, 'Go and completely destroy those wicked people, the Amalekites. Wage war against them until you have wiped them out.' Why did you not obey the Lord? Why did you pounce on the plunder and do evil in the eyes of the Lord?"

"But I did obey the Lord," Saul said. "I went on the mission the Lord assigned me. I completely destroyed the Amalekites and brought back Agag their king. The soldiers took sheep and cattle from the plunder, the best of what was devoted to God, in order to sacrifice them to the Lord your God at Gilgal.

But Samuel replied: "Does the Lord delight in burnt offerings and sacrifices as much as in obeying the Lord? To obey is better than sacrifice, and to heed is better than the fat of rams … Because you have rejected the word of the Lord, he has rejected you as king." (NIV)

D. Insecurity (Saul's Fatal Flaw)

- 1 Samuel 15:24 // Then Saul said to Samuel, "I have sinned. I violated the Lord's command and your instructions. I was afraid of the men, and so I gave in to them." (NIV)

- Saul craved men's approval more than carrying out the Lord's instructions.

E. Keeping Up Appearances

- 1 Samuel 15:30 // Saul replied, "I have sinned. But please honor me before the elders of my people and before Israel. Come back with me so that I may worship the Lord your God." (NIV)

- Instead of genuinely repenting and offering the sacrifice of a broken and contrite heart, Saul's go-to was the show of a burnt offering and to be seen worshiping with Samuel, a real man of integrity.

- Samuel was reluctant but finally agreed to worship with Saul.

V. TALL, DARK, AND TORMENTED

A. Saul was on a tragic downward spiral, and Samuel mourned for him.

B. The rest of his story, including his tragic end, is woven together with the man who would be the successor to the throne—a man after God's own heart.

TALK ABOUT IT

1. Why do you think we have an unhealthy attraction to external appearances? How can we begin to shift the culture?

2. Have you ever disobeyed God out of the fear of what others would think? Explain.

3. Selective Obedience says, "It's okay if I didn't do that because I did this!" What are some examples of selective obedience today, generally and personally?

4. Insecurity, as well as Pride and Arrogance, are in the list of Saul's character flaws. How can someone who is insecure also display pride and arrogance?

5. Samuel said to Saul, "To obey is better than sacrifice." What does that mean to you? How does understanding this principle elevate the way you worship and live?

NOTES

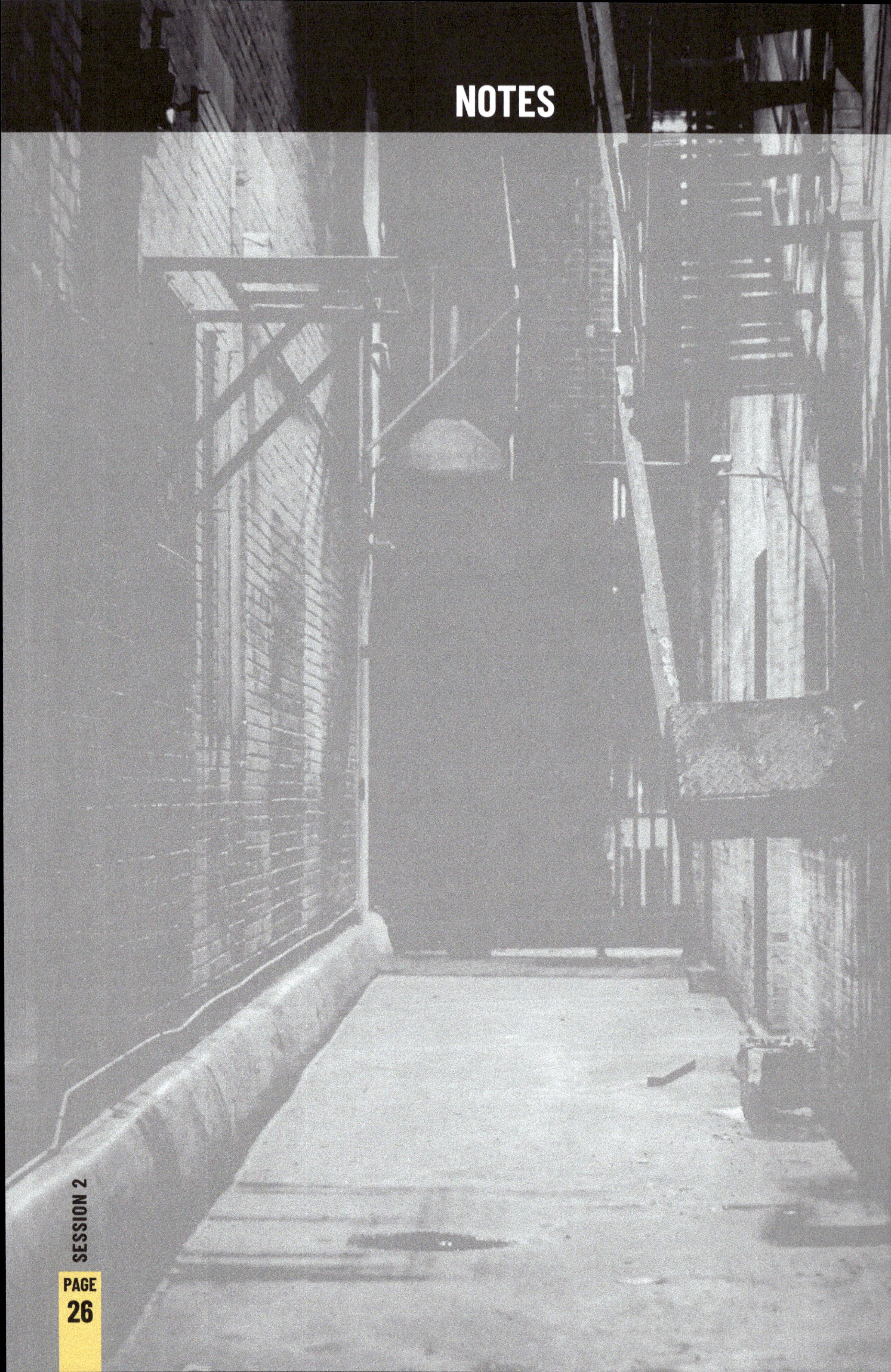

3

A MAN
AFTER GOD'S OWN HEART

GOOD
PEOPLE
BEHAVING
BADLY

A MAN AFTER GOD'S OWN HEART

I. A PROBLEM WITH THE CROWN

   A. Saul was the popular choice of the people.

- He was described as tall and more handsome than any of the sons of Israel.

   B. Saul was blatantly disobedient to God.

- Samuel had the difficult job of informing Saul that he would be replaced.

- 1 Samuel 13:14 // But now, your kingdom will not endure. The Lord has sought out a man after his own heart and appointed him ruler of his people because you have not kept the Lord's command. (NIV)

II. A NEW KING IS REVEALED

   A. God sent Samuel to meet a man named Jesse in Bethlehem and to identify and anoint one of his sons who would be the future king.

- Samuel was impressed by what he saw, but God adjusted his aim to what matters most.

1 Samuel 16:7 // Do not consider his appearance or his height, for I have rejected him. The Lord does not look at the things people look at. **People look at the outward appearance, but the Lord looks at the heart. (NIV)**

B. David, the youngest of the eight sons, had been left to tend the sheep.

- He was Mr. Irrelevant. They had to send someone out to the field to get him.

- 1 Samuel 16:12 // He was glowing with health and had a fine appearance and handsome features. (NIV)

- David's outward glow and handsome features were eclipsed by what was in his heart.

C. Samuel anoints David as Israel's future king.

- 1 Samuel 16:13 // So Samuel took the horn of oil and anointed him in the presence of his brothers, and from that day on, the Spirit of the Lord came powerfully upon David. (NIV)

- The Spirit of the Lord came powerfully upon David, but it was the opposite for King Saul.

REMEMBER: In the Old Testament, the Spirit of God came upon people and briefly empowered them for a purpose. Since Pentecost in the New Testament, the Holy Spirit now lives in us and never leaves us because of God's grace through our faith.

D. Extreme conditions require extreme measures.

- Because of his pattern of disobedience, continually rejecting God's Word, the Spirit of the Lord was removed from Saul, and an evil spirit was allowed to torment him.

- 1 Timothy 1:18-20 // … Fight the battle well, holding on to faith and a good conscience, which some have rejected and so have suffered shipwreck with regard to the faith. Among them are Hymenaeus and Alexander, whom I have handed over to Satan to be taught not to blaspheme. (NIV)

III. GOD CONNECTS THE PATH OF DAVID WITH THE PATH OF SAUL

A. Multiple times in the story of Saul and David, we see Saul's severe mood swings from apathy and depression to raging temper and paranoia.

- Saul's attendants suggested that they find someone who could play the lyre to comfort him when the evil spirit tormented him.

- 1 Samuel 16:18 // I have seen a son of Jesse of Bethlehem who knows how to play the lyre. He is a brave man and a warrior … **And the Lord is with him.** (NIV)

- David's music calmed the king when he was tormented.

- Saul also made David one of his armor-bearers.

B. David and Goliath.

- David was appalled by Goliath's taunts and volunteered to fight him.

- David's brothers and King Saul saw David as young and inexperienced.

- 1 Samuel 17:34-37 // David said to Saul, "Your servant has been keeping his father's sheep. When a lion or a bear came and carried off a sheep from the flock, I went after it, struck it, and rescued the sheep from its mouth. When it turned on me, I seized it by its hair, struck it, and killed it. Your servant has killed both the lion and the bear. This uncircumcised Philistine will be like one of them because he has defied the armies of the living God. The Lord who rescued me from the paw of the lion and the paw of the bear will rescue me from the hand of this Philistine." (NIV)

- David spotlighted the Lord who was with him in the past and who he was certain would be with him as he faced Goliath.

- After David kills Goliath, he stays with Saul and doesn't return to his family.

IV. JEALOUSY AND PARANOIA

A. David was so successful that Saul gave him a high rank in his army.

- The people of Israel and Judah loved David, singing songs like, "Saul has slain his thousands, and David his ten thousands."

- 1 Samuel 18:8-9 // Saul was very angry. This refrain displeased him greatly. "They have credited David with tens of thousands," he thought, "but me with only thousands. What more can he get but the kingdom?" And from that time on Saul kept a close eye on David. (NIV)

B. Saul was afraid because the Lord had departed from him, but the Spirit of the Lord was clearly on David.

- Every decision and assignment Saul gave David was driven by jealousy, which turned into hatred in the hopes that David would be killed in battle.

C. Saul continued on a downward spiral until he and his sons were killed in a bloody battle on Mount Gilboa.

- When David learned the tragic news, he ordered the people to join him in a lament, recorded in 2 Samuel 1.

D. It was not a smooth transition of power.

- 2 Samuel 3:1 // The war between the house of Saul and the house of David lasted a long time. David grew stronger and stronger, while the house of Saul grew weaker and weaker. (NIV)

- David was king over Judah for seven and a half years. He was finally recognized and anointed king over all of Israel and Judah when he was thirty years old.

- David had a winning record and a high approval rating, but he didn't know how to be successful in his success.

V. DAVID AND BATHSHEBA

A. A shift in David's leadership.

- 2 Samuel 11:1 // In the spring, at the time when kings go off to war, David sent Joab out with the king's men and the whole Israelite army ... But David remained in Jerusalem. (NIV)

- Delegating responsibility is good, but disengaging is dangerous.

B. A look turns into lust, and lust turns into adultery.

C. A royal cover-up.

- David's plan to deceive Uriah fails, and now he is desperate.

- 2 Samuel 11:14-15 // In the morning, David wrote a letter to Joab and sent it with Uriah. In it, he wrote, "Put Uriah out in front where the fighting is fiercest. Then withdraw from him so he will be struck down and die." (NIV)

- Uriah is killed in battle, and David is now guilty of adultery and murder.

D. David marries Bathsheba.

- Clearly, David was not behaving like a man after God's own heart.

- 2 Samuel 11:27 // The thing David had done displeased the Lord.

Regardless of our approval rating, the opinion of our friends, or how convinced we are that our actions are justified, if God is not pleased, we are in serious trouble.

TALK ABOUT IT

1. God told Samuel, *"The Lord does not look at the things people look at. People look at the outward appearance, but the Lord looks at the heart."* How can we focus on the heart in communication with our spouse, children, friends, and even strangers?

2. When David made his case before King Saul for a chance to face Goliath (1 Samuel 17:34-37), how did he display confidence without being arrogant? How can we do the same?

3. When David learned of the deaths of King Saul and Jonathan, he ordered the people to join him in a lament, recorded in 2 Samuel 1:17-27. How does this honorable act display that David was a man after God's own heart? How can we apply this principle today?

4. What do David's choices with Bathsheba and Uriah tell us about our potential for epic failure? 1 Corinthians 10:12 says, *"If you think you are standing firm, be careful that you don't fall."* How does that apply?

5. Cover-ups are common today. What is a better choice, and why is it a challenge?

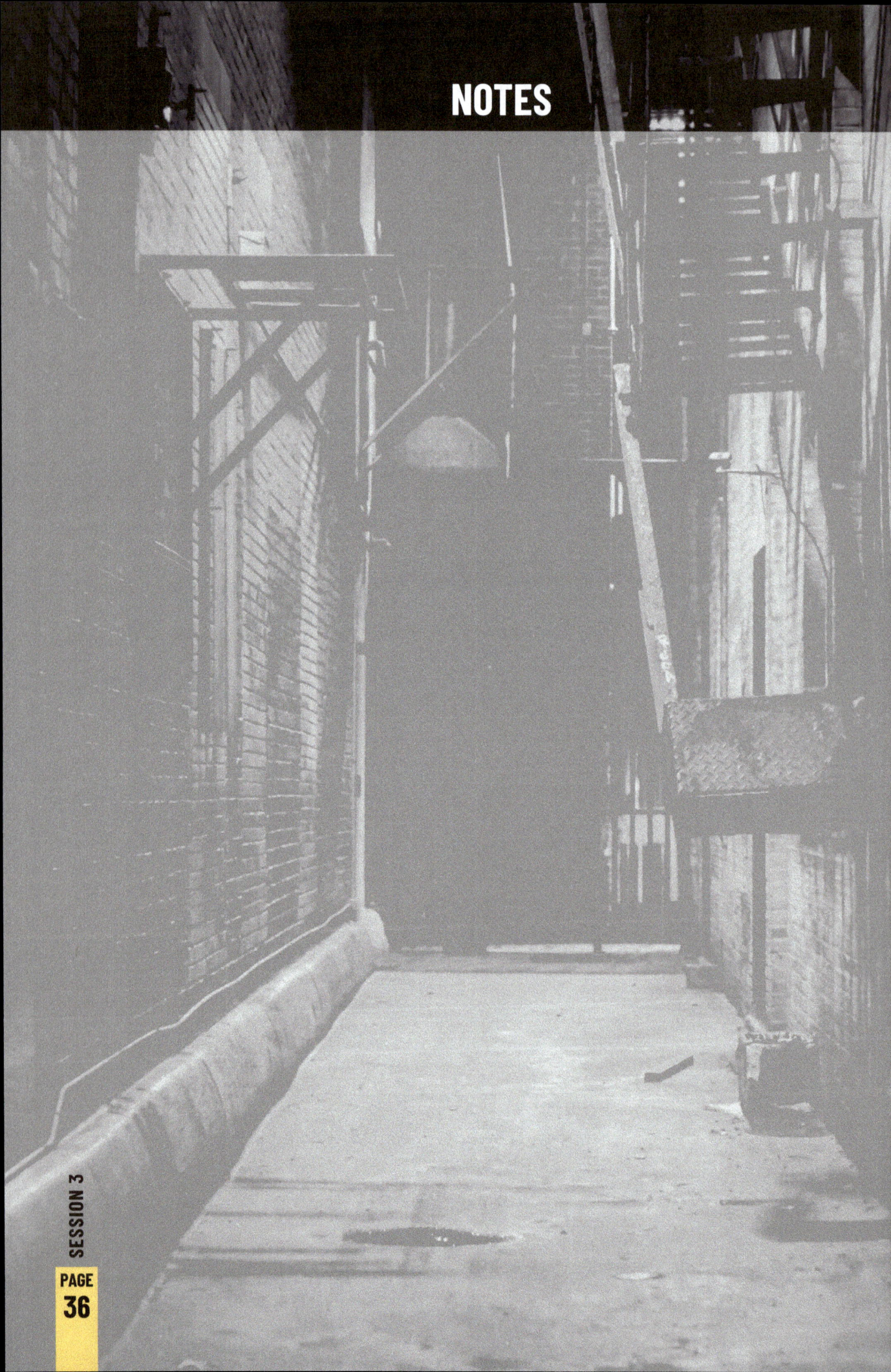

4

RIGHT THINKING
ABOUT WRONG BEHAVIOR

GOOD
PEOPLE
BEHAVING
BADLY

> **2 SAMUEL 11:27**
>
> After the time of mourning was over, David had her brought to his house,
> and she became his wife and bore him a son.
>
> But the thing David had done displeased the Lord.

I. DAVID AND NATHAN

A. A formal indictment packaged in a parable.

- David expresses his anger about another man's bad behavior:

  2 Samuel 12:5-6 // David burned with anger against the man and said to Nathan, "As surely as the Lord lives, the man who did this must die! He must pay for that lamb four times over because he did such a thing and had no pity." (NIV)

- Nathan delivers God's indictment against David:

  2 Samuel 12:7-10 // Then Nathan said to David, "You are the man! This is what the Lord, the God of Israel, says: 'I anointed you king over Israel, and I delivered you from the hand of Saul. I gave your master's house to you and your master's wives into your arms. I gave you all Israel and Judah. And if all this had been too little, I would have given you even more.

  "'Why did you despise the word of the Lord by doing what is evil in his eyes? You struck down Uriah the Hittite with the sword and took his wife to be your own. You killed him with the sword of the Ammonites. Now, therefore, the sword will never depart from your house, because you despised me and took the wife of Uriah the Hittite to be your own.'" (NIV)

- The reality of God's forgiveness and the damage caused by sin.

B. David responds with brokenness and humility.

- 2 Samuel 12:13-14 // Then David said to Nathan, "I have sinned against the Lord."

  Nathan replied, "The Lord has taken away your sin. You are not going to die. But because by doing this you have shown utter contempt for the Lord, the son born to you will die." (NIV)

- David prays and fasts > His son dies > David worships God.

- There is a shift back to the man after God's own heart.

II. 3 LEVELS OF CONFESSION AND REPENTANCE

A. PRIVATE

- If only you and God know about it, that's as far as it needs to go unless God leads you to share it to strengthen the church. (Be sure God is leading you!)

- Confess and repent in a way that glorifies God, helps others, and doesn't focus on your sin or call attention to your acts of repentance.

B. PERSONAL

- If the sin is personal between you and another person or persons, start privately before God. Then, ask Him to guide you as you confess and repent personally before others who have been affected.

- Confess and repent in a way that glorifies God, helps others, and doesn't focus on your sin or call attention to your acts of repentance.

C. PUBLIC

- If the ripple effect of sin has spread beyond you and God to another person or persons and has now, or will, become public knowledge, start privately before God, then go to the person or persons who were directly affected.

- Ask God to guide you in addressing it publicly. Pray about what steps need to be taken, not to save your career but to genuinely accept responsibility with humility and brokenness.

- Confess and repent in a way that glorifies God, helps others, and doesn't focus on your sin or call attention to your acts of repentance.

III. PSALM 51 – A PUBLIC DECLARATION OF CONFESSION AND REPENTANCE

PSALM 51:1-2

Have mercy on me, O God, according to your unfailing love. According to your great compassion, blot out my **transgressions**. Wash away all my **iniquity** and cleanse me from my **sin**.

A. David uses three words to describe his bad behavior:

- **Transgression describes outright rebellion**—willingly stepping over God's boundaries. It's when something is believed to be more important than doing what's right.

- **Iniquity expresses our moral impurity.** We transgress because we have iniquity inside us. We've been justified before God because of Jesus, but our sinful nature hasn't been eradicated yet.

- **Sin is about our gross inability to measure up**—like pulling the arrow back as far as you can, and it always falls short. And our arrows don't just miss the mark on the target—they can't even reach the target.

IV. THE DAMAGE CAUSED BY SIN

A. Sin makes us feel dirty.

- Psalm 51:7 // Cleanse me with hyssop, and I will be clean. Wash me, and I will be whiter than snow. (NIV)

- Psalm 51:9 // Hide your face from my sins and blot out all my iniquity. (NIV)

B. Sin hinders our vision.

- Psalm 51:3 // For I know my transgressions and my sin is always before me. (NIV)

C. Sin dulls our hearing.

- Psalm 51:8 // Let me hear joy and gladness … (NIV)

D. Sin crushes our confidence.

- Psalm 51:8 // … Let the bones you have crushed rejoice. (NIV)

E. Sin makes us question our identity and even doubt our salvation.

- Psalm 51:11 // Do not cast me from your presence or take your Holy Spirit from me. (NIV)

- We have a new identity because of Jesus.

  John 1:12-13 // To all who did receive him, to those who believed in his name, he gave the right to become children of God—children born not of natural descent, nor of human decision or a husband's will, but born of God. (NIV)

- There is nothing we can do to earn our salvation or lose it.

  Ephesians 2:8-9 // It is by grace you have been saved, through faith—and this is not from yourselves, it is the gift of God—not by works so that no one can boast. (NIV)

F. Sin robs us of the joy of our salvation.

- Psalm 51:12 // Restore to me the joy of your salvation and grant me a willing spirit to sustain me. (NIV)

G. Sin undermines our influence.

- Psalm 51:13 // Then I will teach transgressors your ways so that sinners will turn back to you. (NIV)

H. Sin hinders our worship.

- Psalm 51:15 // Open my lips, Lord, and my mouth will declare your praise. (NIV)

- Psalm 51:16 // You do not delight in sacrifice, or I would bring it. You do not take pleasure in burnt offerings. (NIV)

V. 3 KEY REALITIES

A. All sin is vertical.

- Psalm 51:4 // Against you, and you only, have I sinned and done what is evil in your sight. So you are right in your verdict and justified when you judge. (NIV)

B. My biggest problem is me.

- Psalm 51:5 // Surely I was sinful at birth, sinful from the time my mother conceived me. (NIV)

C. My greatest need is something I can't give myself.

- Psalm 51:10 // Create in me a pure heart, O God, and renew a steadfast spirit within me. (NIV)

VI. FINAL THOUGHTS

A. Unlike King Saul, David's repentance was real.

- Psalm 51:17 // My sacrifice, O God, is a broken spirit. A broken and contrite heart you, God, will not despise. (NIV)

B. Because of God's grace, David's life was not defined by his bad behavior.

- Psalm 78:70-72 // He chose David, his servant, and took him from the sheep pens. From tending the sheep, he brought him to be the shepherd of his people Jacob, of Israel his inheritance. And David shepherded them with integrity of heart. With skillful hands, he led them. (NIV)

TALK ABOUT IT

1. Have you ever committed a transgression (outright rebellion) against God? What were the circumstances and the consequences?

2. Have you experienced the three levels of confession and repentance: private, personal, and public? Explain.

3. Review the list of 8 Damages Caused By Sin. Which ones do you identify with?

4. What are your thoughts on the 3 Key Realities?—(1) All sin is vertical, (2) My biggest problem is me, and (3) My greatest need is something I can't give myself. Are they difficult to admit? If so, why?

5. How have you seen real repentance in action?

NOTES

You will never make yourself feel you are a sinner because there is a mechanism in you as a result of sin that will always be defending you ... We are all on good terms with ourselves.

– Martyn Lloyd-Jones

5

BURNOUT

GOOD
PEOPLE
BEHAVING
BADLY

BURNOUT

I. INTRODUCTION

A. Elijah was a mighty prophet about ninety years after the reign of King David.

- The kingdom had split into the northern kingdom of Israel and the southern kingdom of Judah because of the poor leadership of Solomon's son, Rehoboam.

- Ahab was king of Israel, and he did more evil in the eyes of the Lord than any of those before him.

- Under Ahab's leadership, the nation had turned away from the Lord to worship Baal.

B. Elijah is first mentioned in 1 Kings 17, where he declared a drought as a penalty for Israel's evil behavior.

C. God's protection, provision, and preparation.

- God sent Elijah to the Kerith Ravine, where ravens brought him food twice a day, and he drank from the brook.

- When the brook dried up, God sent Elijah to the town of Zarephath where a widow fed and cared for him from a flour jar that would not be used up and a jug of oil that would not run dry.

- When the widow's son became ill and died, Elijah raised him from the dead.

- 1 Kings 17:24 // Then the woman said to Elijah, "Now I know that you are a man of God and that the word of the Lord from your mouth is the truth." (NIV)

II. THE SHOWDOWN ON MOUNT CARMEL

A. The Challenge.

- 1 Kings 18:21-24 // Elijah went before the people and said, "How long will you waver between two opinions? If the Lord is God, follow him. But if Baal is God, follow him."

  But the people said nothing.

  Then Elijah said to them, "I am the only one of the Lord's prophets left, but Baal has four hundred and fifty prophets. Get two bulls for us. Let Baal's prophets choose one for themselves, and let them cut it into pieces and put it on the wood but not set fire to it. I will prepare the other bull and put it on the wood but not set fire to it. Then you call on the name of your god, and I will call on the name of the Lord. The god who answers by fire—he is God."

  Then all the people said, "What you say is good." (NIV)

B. From morning until evening, the prophets of Baal shouted, danced, cried out, and even cut themselves with no response from their god. (1 Kings 18:25-29)

C. The Fire of the Lord.

- Elijah repaired the altar of the Lord, incorporating twelve stones, one for each of the twelve tribes of Israel.

- Elijah dug a deep trench around the altar and instructed the people to fill four jars with water and pour it over the wood three times.

- 1 Kings 18:36-39 // The prophet Elijah stepped forward and prayed: "Lord, the God of Abraham, Isaac, and Israel, let it be known today that you are God in Israel and that I am your servant and have done all these things at your command. Answer me, Lord, answer me, so these people will know that you, Lord, are God and that you are turning their hearts back again."

  Then the fire of the Lord fell and burned up the sacrifice, the wood, the stones and the soil, and also licked up the water in the trench.

  When all the people saw this, they fell prostrate and cried, "The Lord—he is God! The Lord—he is God!" (NIV)

- Elijah prophesied rain, ending a three-and-a-half-year drought.

- God gave Elijah supernatural strength to outrun Ahab's chariot.

  1 Kings 18:46 // The power of the Lord came on Elijah and, tucking his cloak into his belt, he ran ahead of Ahab all the way to Jezreel. (NIV)

III. BURNOUT

A. Jezebel's death threat was too much for Elijah.

- 1 Kings 19:4-5 // He came to a broom bush, sat down under it, and prayed that he might die. "I have had enough, Lord," he said. "Take my life! I am no better than my ancestors." Then he lay down under the bush and fell asleep. (NIV)

B. Elijah was physically exhausted, emotionally drained, and spiritually depleted.

C. Things we need to understand and practice before (or when) we hit the wall:

- Psalm 23:4 // Even though I walk through the darkest valley, I will fear no evil, for you are with me. Your rod and your staff, they comfort me. (NIV)

- Philippians 4:13 // I can do all things through him who strengthens me.

- Psalm 42:11 // Why, my soul, are you downcast? Why so disturbed within me? Put your hope in God, for I will yet praise him, my Savior and my God. (NIV)

- Matthew 26:41 // … The spirit is willing, but the flesh is weak. (NIV)

C. The danger of leading on empty.

Long-term stress depletes the normal fuel produced biochemically by hormones and secreted into the brain and nervous system … Once these serotonins are exhausted, adrenaline has to be produced to take their place. Soon, an addiction to adrenaline puts a demand on your body for greater amounts. Adrenaline is secreted at increasing rates, and your body becomes dependent on this powerful chemical to meet deadlines, get reports ready, and rise to the expectations of others—or your own.

Adrenaline addiction is an emotional suicide that will slowly progress and may be difficult to detect … Should you continue to run on adrenaline, it will destroy your system. You will burn out sooner on the inside than you're able to see on the outside. The fuel of adrenaline that keeps your engines running in the beginning will turn on you and destroy you in the end … If not recognized, stress will precede burnout, and burnout is often accompanied by a super-sized helping of depression.[2]   - Wayne Cordeiro

_____

[2] Wayne Cordeiro, "Leading On Empty: Refilling Your Tank And Renewing Your Passion."

D. There is a difference between isolation and solitude.

> The days I spent at the monastery taught me the difference between solitude and isolation. They may contain similar characteristics, but in reality, they are worlds apart. Solitude is a chosen separation for refining your soul. Isolation is what you crave when you neglect the first ... Solitude is a healthy and prescriptive discipline; isolation is a symptom of emotional depletion.[3]
>
> – Wayne Cordeiro

IV. REPLENISHED AND REFRESHED

A. Elijah needed physical sustenance and rest.

*   1 Kings 19:5-9 // All at once, an angel touched him and said, "Get up and eat." He looked around, and there by his head was some bread baked over hot coals and a jar of water. He ate and drank and then lay down again.

    The angel of the Lord came back a second time and touched him and said, "Get up and eat, for the journey is too much for you." So he got up and ate and drank. Strengthened by that food, he traveled forty days and forty nights until he reached Horeb, the mountain of God. There, he went into a cave and spent the night. (NIV)

We need to identify what fills our tank and what drains it.

B. Elijah needed a deeper understanding and more intimate experience with God.

---

[3] Wayne Cordeiro, "Leading On Empty: Refilling Your Tank And Renewing Your Passion,"

- 1 Kings 19:11-13 // The Lord said, "Go out and stand on the mountain in the presence of the Lord, for the Lord is about to pass by."

  Then a great and powerful wind tore the mountains apart and shattered the rocks before the Lord, but the Lord was not in the wind. After the wind there was an earthquake, but the Lord was not in the earthquake. After the earthquake came a fire, but the Lord was not in the fire. And after the fire came a gentle whisper. When Elijah heard it, he pulled his cloak over his face and went out and stood at the mouth of the cave. When Elijah heard it, he pulled his cloak over his face and went out and stood at the mouth of the cave.

  Then a voice said to him, "What are you doing here, Elijah?" (NIV)

C. Tune in to the gentle whisper of God.

- Tell God whatever is on your mind and weighing heavy on your heart.

  1 Peter 5:7 // Cast all your anxiety on him because he cares for you. (NIV)

- Follow the example of Jesus.

  Luke 5:16 // Jesus often withdrew to lonely places and prayed. (NIV)

We need to develop a habit of spending time in solitary places, which can become sacred places where we learn to listen to the gentle whisper of God.

TALK ABOUT IT

1. What lessons do you think Elijah learned from his experiences in the Kerith Ravine and the widow's home? How could those lessons help you today?

2. Elijah was clearly outnumbered on Mount Carmel. There were 450 prophets of Baal and 400 prophets of Asherah on one side and Elijah on the other. Have you ever faced what seemed like insurmountable odds and experienced God's presence and power to accomplish His purpose? Explain.

3. Elijah hit the wall after the epic showdown on Mount Carmel. He was physically exhausted, emotionally drained, and spiritually depleted. Have you experienced that kind of burnout? Explain.

4. Wayne Cordeiro said, "The fuel of adrenaline that keeps your engines running in the beginning will turn on you and destroy you in the end … If not recognized, stress will precede burnout, and burnout is often accompanied by a super-sized helping of depression." How can we recognize that dangerous pattern?

5. Elijah needed a deeper understanding and more intimate experience with God. We need the same. Talk about the difference between seeking isolation vs. our need for solitude. What are you doing (or what do you need to do) to experience a healthy habit of solitude with God?

NOTES

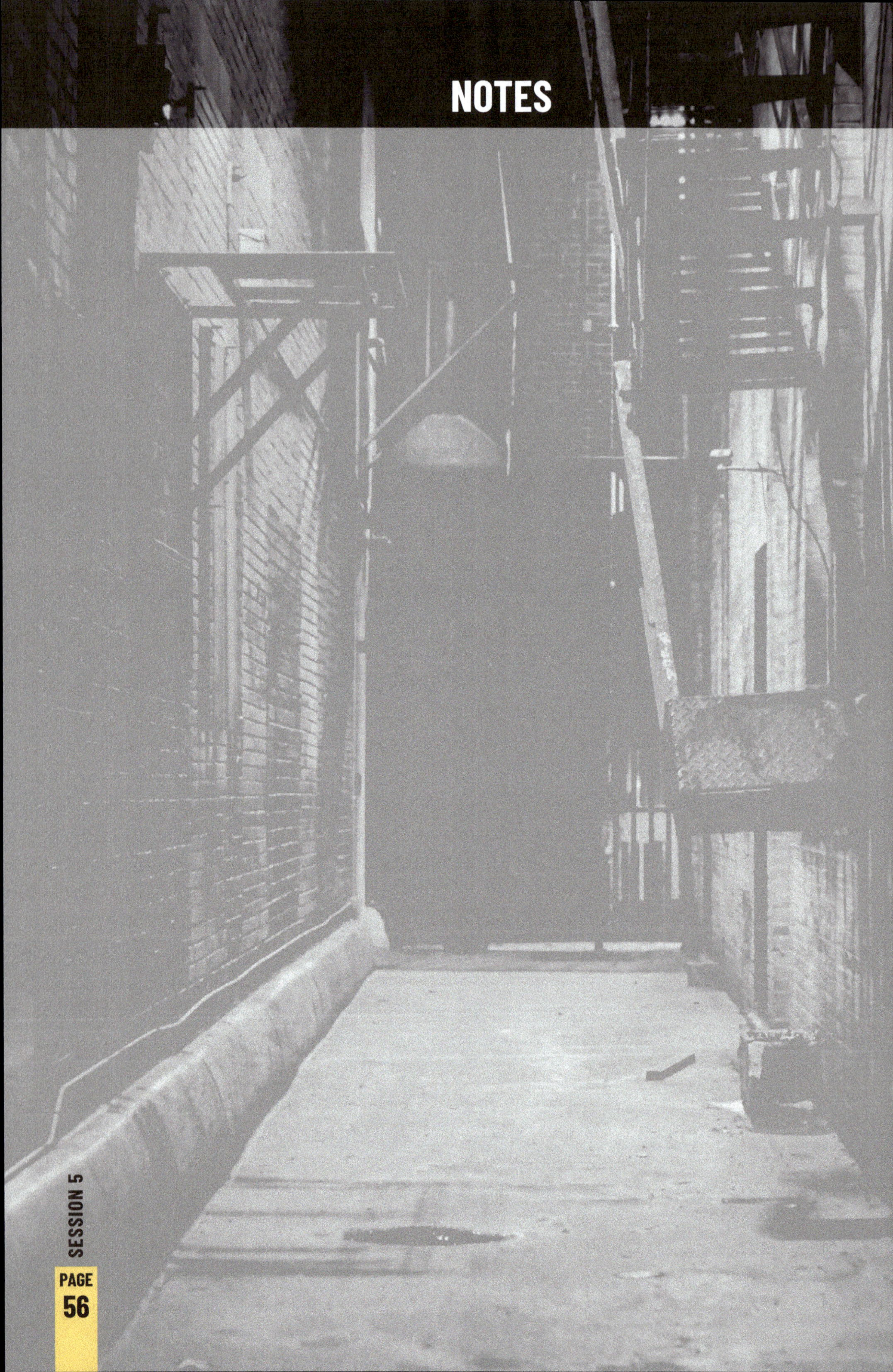

6

UNDERNEATH IT ALL

GOOD
PEOPLE
BEHAVING
BADLY

I. RECAP AND INTRODUCTION

A. Cautionary tales in this series so far: a grumbling nation, the insecurity and selective obedience of Israel's first king, the epic failure of Israel's second king, and the burnout of a mighty prophet.

B. The purpose of this series is to help us develop habits that are preventive, not just medicinal—to be proactive rather than reactive.

C. Bad behavior is the acting out of a deeper problem.

- Luke 6:45 // A good man brings good things out of the good stored up in his heart, and an evil man brings evil things out of the evil stored up in his heart. For the mouth speaks what the heart is full of. (NIV)

- Beneath the symptoms on the surface are the root causes of bad behavior.

II. A WARNING FROM THE PROPHET JEREMIAH

A. God gave Jeremiah a mission to tear down and build up.

- Jeremiah 1:10 // Today, I appoint you over nations and kingdoms to uproot and tear down, to destroy and overthrow, to build and to plant. (NIV)

B. God's indictment against His people.

- Jeremiah 2:5-9 // "What fault did your ancestors find in me that they strayed so far from me? They followed worthless idols and became worthless themselves" … "Therefore, I bring charges against you again," declares the Lord. "And I will bring charges against your children's children." (NIV)

- What lies underneath it all is an inadequate view of who we are and who God is.

With our loss of the sense of Majesty has come the further loss of religious awe and consciousness of the divine presence. ... The decline of the knowledge of the holy has brought on our troubles. A rediscovery of the majesty of God will go a long way toward curing them.[4]   – A.W. Tozer

C. There were two charges against God's people.

- Jeremiah 2:13 // My people have committed two sins: They have forsaken me, the spring of living water, and have dug their own cisterns, broken cisterns that cannot hold water. (NIV)

- The first sin was forsaking God.

- The second sin was replacing God with broken cisterns.

"Broken Cisterns" is a metaphor for idols. For a cistern to function properly, it had to be waterproof. If it cracked and couldn't be repaired, it became useless.

This is why the actions of the people of Israel were so ridiculous. They had replaced God with idols that were like cisterns that couldn't hold water. They had exchanged their glorious God for worthless idols.

---

[4] A.W. Tozer, "The Knowledge of the Holy"

III. A FRAMEWORK FOR DEALING WITH IDOLS

(Much of the content in this section is adapted from *33 The Series, Volume 3: A Man and His Traps*.[5])

A. Idolatry is when we allow anything other than God to become the center of our heart's true happiness, contentment, meaning, identity, purpose, or security.

> Idolatry is always the reason we ever do anything wrong. Why do we ever lie, fail to love, keep promises, or live unselfishly? ... The specific answer is always that there is something besides Jesus Christ that you feel you must have to be happy, something that is more important to your heart than God. The secret to change is always to identify the idols of the heart.
>
> – Tim Keller

B. There are 3 things we need to know about idols:

- An idol can be anything, even a good thing.

- Idolatry is built on a lie.

- Idols come from legitimate desires expressed in inappropriate ways.

IV. THE 3 IDOLS UNDERNEATH OUR BAD BEHAVIOR

A. CONTROL

- **THE LIE:** If I can maintain influence or mastery over this situation, these people, my performance, my schedule, my income—or whatever—then I'll be okay, content, strong, and safe.

---

[5] Adapted from "33 The Series, Volume 3: A Man and His Traps," authenticmanhood.com

- You're driven by certainty and dominance.

- Your biggest fear is instability or weakness.

B. SIGNIFICANCE

- **THE LIE:** If this person, this social group, or the colleagues in my profession find me worthy of attention or love—if they acknowledge my value or greatness, then I'll be worthy, important, and acceptable.

- You're driven by affirmation and being made to feel important.

- Your biggest fear is rejection or humiliation.

C. COMFORT

- **THE LIE:** If I can maintain physical ease or relaxation, if life can be laid back, if I can stay away from stress or responsibility—if I can experience some pleasure or enjoyment in the moment, then life will be more fulfilling, easy, fun, or thrilling.

- You're driven by a fear of stress and responsibility.

- You may have a tendency toward quitting and laziness, which you've tried to spin as just being laid back.

V. ATTACK THE ROOTS

A. We need a heart change.

- Jeremiah 17:9 // The heart is deceitful above all things and beyond cure. Who can understand it? (NIV)

- Mark 7:21-22 // From within, out of the heart of man, come evil thoughts, sexual immorality, theft, murder, adultery, coveting, wickedness, deceit, sensuality, envy, slander, pride, foolishness. (NIV)

- Behavior modification without heart change is dangerous. On the surface, it looks like holiness, but it hides the deeper issues.

B. THE BATTLE PLAN[6]

■ ADMIT THE STRUGGLE

■ IDENTIFY THE LIE

■ REPLACE WITH THE TRUTH

---

[6] Adapted from "33 The Series, Volume 3: A Man and His Traps," authenticmanhood.com

VI. BUILD AND PLANT

Jeremiah 17:7-8 // Blessed is the one who trusts in the Lord, whose confidence is in him. They will be like a tree planted by the water that sends out its roots by the stream. It does not fear when heat comes. Its leaves are always green. It has no worries in a year of drought and never fails to bear fruit. (NIV)

TALK ABOUT IT

1. It's easy to condemn the actions of a nation that had forsaken God and replaced Him with worthless idols. But how do we do the same thing today?

2. We defined idolatry as allowing anything other than God to become the center of our heart's true happiness, contentment, meaning, identity, purpose, or security. Why is it difficult to recognize idolatry in our own lives?

3. We identified three idols that are underneath all of our bad behavior: CONTROL, SIGNIFICANCE, and COMFORT. Which one(s) do you struggle with the most?

4. Review the lie(s) you're believing when you give in to any one of these idols. Why do you think the lies are more appealing than the truth of God's Word? What can you do to shift the appeal?

5. What do you need to do to implement the Battle Plan—Admit The Struggle, Identify The Lie, Replace With The Truth? How can this become a proactive practice in your life?

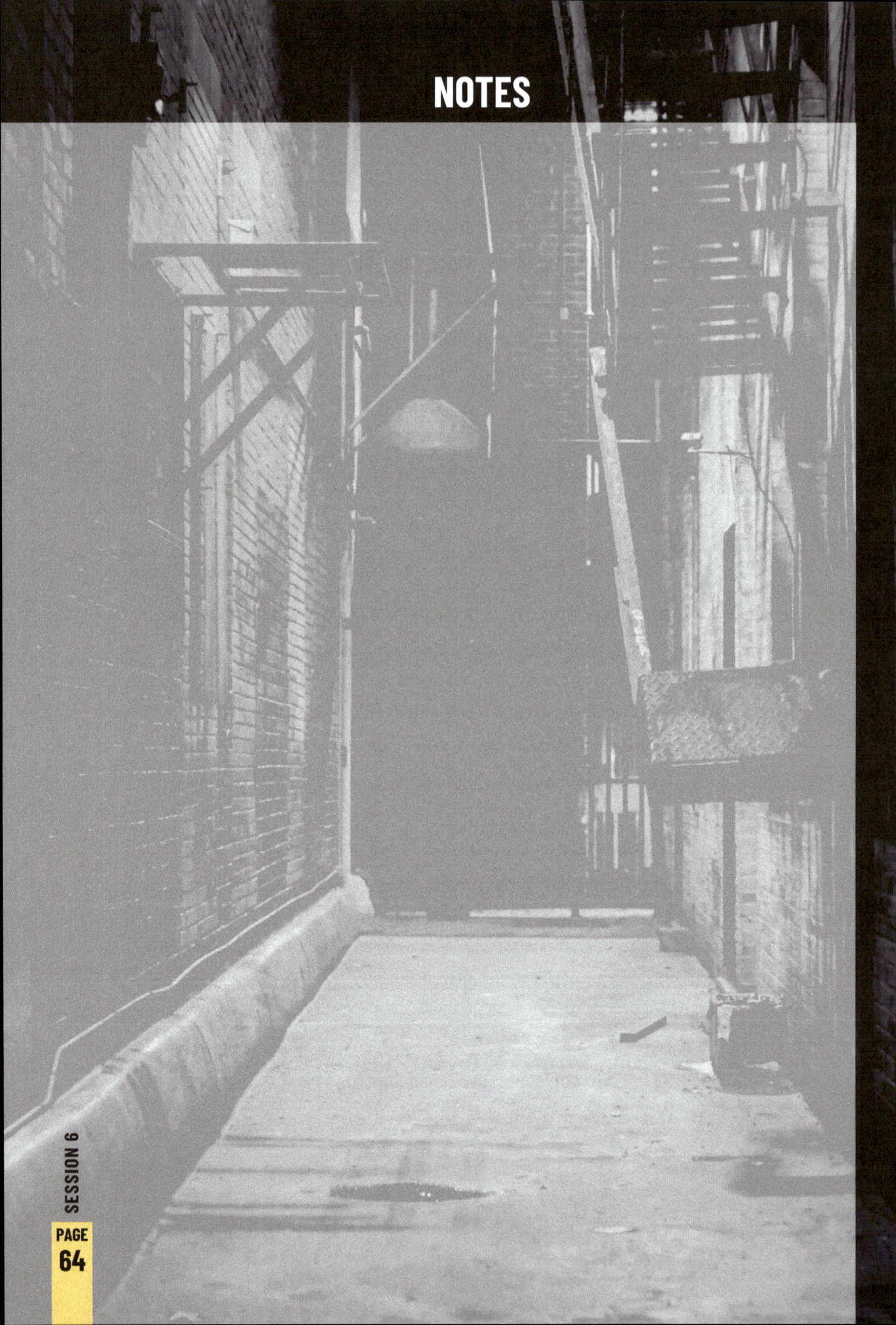

NOTES

7

REPEAT OFFENDERS

GOOD PEOPLE BEHAVING BADLY

REPEAT OFFENDERS

I. SAUL OF THE NEW TESTAMENT

A. In religious circles, Saul was known to be a good and righteous man.

- Philippians 3:4-6 // If someone else thinks they have reasons to put confidence in the flesh, I have more: circumcised on the eighth day, of the people of Israel, of the tribe of Benjamin, a Hebrew of Hebrews. In regard to the law, a Pharisee. As for zeal, persecuting the church. As for righteousness based on the law, faultless. (NIV)

- The Pharisees were a society of scholars who emphasized the study of God's Law. They were very pious and sincere. However, when it came to Jesus, they were sincerely wrong.

B. On his way to Damascus, Saul experienced a life-altering revelation.

- Acts 9:1-6 // Meanwhile, Saul was still breathing out murderous threats against the Lord's disciples. He went to the high priest and asked him for letters to the synagogues in Damascus, so that if he found any there who belonged to the Way, whether men or women, he might take them as prisoners to Jerusalem. As he neared Damascus on his journey, suddenly, a light from heaven flashed around him. He fell to the ground and heard a voice say to him, "Saul, Saul, why do you persecute me?"

  "Who are you, Lord?" Saul asked.

  "I am Jesus, whom you are persecuting," he replied. "Now get up and go into the city, and you will be told what you must do." (NIV)

C. Ananias and Barnabas play key roles in Saul's transition.

- Acts 9:15-19 // The Lord said to Ananias, "Go! This man is my chosen instrument to proclaim my name to the Gentiles and their kings and to the people of Israel. I will show him how much he must suffer for my name."

  Then Ananias went to the house and entered it. Placing his hands on Saul, he said, "Brother Saul, the Lord—Jesus, who appeared to you on the road as you were coming here—has sent me so that you may see again and be filled with the Holy Spirit." Immediately, something like scales fell from Saul's eyes, and he could see again. He got up and was baptized, and after taking some food, he regained his strength. (NIV)

- Barnabas encouraged the disciples in Jerusalem to accept Saul.

D. A new reputation, a new name, and a new identity.

- Saul would go from being the chief persecutor of the church to becoming a chief planter of churches with Barnabas.

- Saul became known as Paul the Apostle.

- Philippians 3:7-10 // Whatever were gains to me, I now consider loss for the sake of Christ. What is more, I consider everything a loss because of the surpassing worth of knowing Christ Jesus my Lord, for whose sake I have lost all things. I consider them garbage, that I may gain Christ and be found in him, not having a righteousness of my own that comes from the law, but that which is through faith in Christ … I want to know Christ—yes, to know the power of his resurrection and participation in his sufferings, becoming like him in his death. (NIV)

II. A NEW UNDERSTANDING OF THE LAW

A. Paul explains the origins of sin and righteousness.

- Romans 5:18-19 // Just as one trespass resulted in condemnation for all people, so also one righteous act resulted in justification and life for all people. For just as through the disobedience of the one man, the many were made sinners, so also through the obedience of the one man, the many will be made righteous. (NIV)

- Like Paul, we need to understand that we inherited our sinful nature from Adam.

> Faith in the sacrifice of Jesus for our sins is our only hope of attaining the righteousness God requires and the life we desperately need in place of the death we deserve.

B. Paul explains the purpose of the law and the power of God's grace.

- Romans 5:20-21 // The law was brought in so that the trespass might increase. But where sin increased, grace increased all the more, so that, just as sin reigned in death, so also grace might reign through righteousness to bring eternal life through Jesus Christ our Lord. (NIV)

- The Law reminds us that we could never measure up to God's standard of righteousness.

- God's grace is super-abundant, which means there is no sin too big for God to forgive.

III. HOW WE SEE OURSELVES

A. We are dead to sin and alive to God.

- Romans 6:1-2 // What shall we say, then? Shall we go on sinning so that grace may increase? By no means! We are those who have died to sin. How can we live in it any longer? (NIV)

- Romans 6:11 // … count yourselves dead to sin but alive to God in Christ Jesus. (NIV)

B. We are instruments of righteousness.

- Romans 6:13 // Do not offer any part of yourself to sin as an instrument of wickedness, but rather offer yourselves to God as those who have been brought from death to life. And offer every part of yourself to him as an instrument of righteousness. (NIV)

- Romans 6:14; 18 // Sin shall no longer be your master because you are not under the law but under grace … You have been set free from sin and have become slaves to righteousness. (NIV)

IV. CLOSING THE GAP BETWEEN GOD'S GRACE AND OUR BEHAVIOR

A. In his own words, the Apostle Paul was a repeat offender

- Romans 7:15-19 // I do not understand what I do. For what I want to do, I do not do, but what I hate I do … For I do not do the good I want to do, but the evil I do not want to do—this I keep on doing. (NIV)

B. 6 THINGS WE NEED TO KNOW AND PRACTICE

1. Don't use God's grace as permission to sin.

   - God's grace is unearned and undeserved. It's a free gift, not a free pass.

   - If you truly understand God's mercy and grace, you will not use it as permission to sin.

2. Never surrender to our human condition.

   - When Paul described our tendency to be repeat offenders, his conclusion was not "It is what it is." Remember what he said …

   - Romans 6:1-2 // Shall we go on sinning so that grace may increase? By no means! We are those who have died to sin. How can we live in it any longer? (NIV)

3. Renew your mind.

   - Meditating on God's Word changes the way we act by changing the way we think.

   - Romans 12:2 // … be transformed by the renewing of your mind. (NIV)

4. Take an inventory.

   - Every part of our body can be used for the purpose of wickedness or righteousness.

- Psalm 101:3 // I will not look with approval on anything that is vile.

- James 3: 9-10 // With the tongue, we praise our Lord and Father, and with it, we curse human beings who have been made in God's likeness. Out of the same mouth come praise and cursing. My brothers and sisters, this should not be. (NIV)

5. Understand the battle within.

- Romans 7:21-23 // So I find this law at work: Although I want to do good, evil is right there with me. For in my inner being, I delight in God's law. But I see another law at work in me, waging war against the law of my mind and making me a prisoner of the law of sin at work within me. (NIV)

- We are free from the penalty of sin because of God's grace. One day, we will be eternally free from the presence of sin. But for now, we drift between victory and defeat as we fight against the power of sin.

6. Make an accurate assessment.

- Romans 7:24-25 // What a wretched man I am! Who will rescue me from this body that is subject to death? Thanks be to God, who delivers me through Jesus Christ our Lord! (NIV)

- We can't get the help we need until we have an accurate assessment of ourselves and know the answer to the question, "Who will rescue me from this body that is subject to death?"

V. FINAL THOUGHTS

A. Making an accurate assessment is not a one-and-done exercise.

- Luke 9:23 // Whoever wants to be my disciple must deny themselves and take up their cross **daily** and follow me. (NIV)

TALK ABOUT IT

1. Saul's conversion from a belief in righteousness that comes from the law to righteousness through faith in Christ is a dramatic religion-to-relationship story. What's your story? Share the details of how you put your faith in Jesus.

2. What does God's super-abundant grace (no sin too big for God to forgive) mean to you?

3. How have you seen God's grace abused?

4. "It is what it is." How can that perspective lead us to surrender to our human condition and cause us to be repeat offenders?

5. How does Paul's own admission of being a repeat offender in Romans 7:15-19 help you?

6. Personal Reflection: When you consider God's standard of righteousness, do you see yourself as wretched and unable to measure up? Do you truly believe that Jesus—and Jesus alone—is your only hope? (Romans 7:24-25)

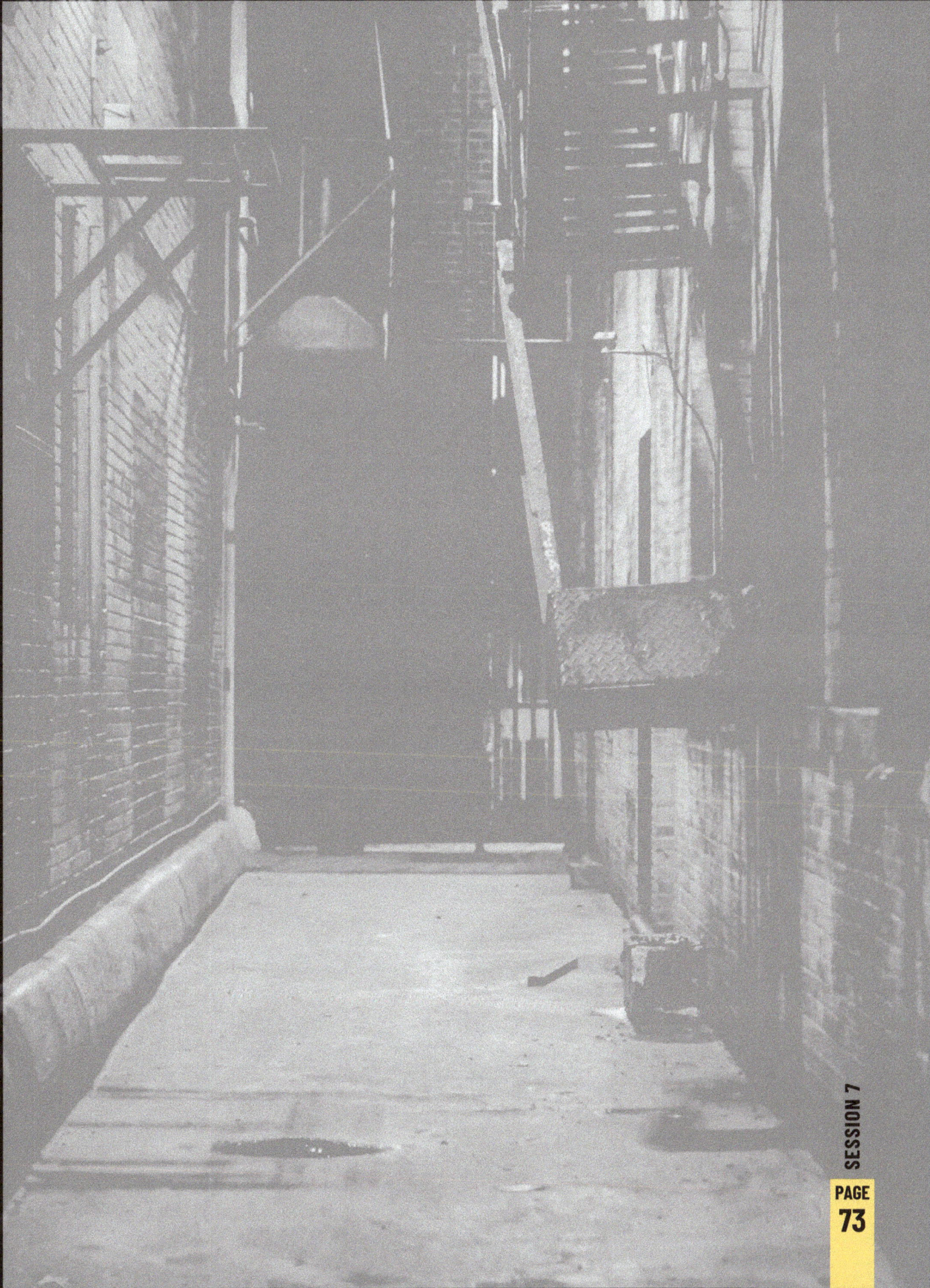

NOTES

8

I'VE GOT THIS

GOOD
PEOPLE
BEHAVING
BADLY

I. FROM A FISHERMAN TO A FOLLOWER

A. Simon and his brother Andrew were fishermen when Jesus called them to follow Him.

- Matthew 4:18-20 // As Jesus was walking beside the Sea of Galilee, he saw two brothers, Simon called Peter and his brother Andrew. They were casting a net into the lake, for they were fishermen. "Come, follow me," Jesus said, "and I will send you out to fish for people." At once, they left their nets and followed him. (NIV)

B. Simon was either right on or way off.

- A rock-solid proclamation.

  Matthew 16:16 // You are the Messiah, the Son of the living God! (NIV)

- Jesus gives Simon a new name.

  Matthew 16:17-18 // Jesus replied, "Blessed are you, Simon son of Jonah, for this was not revealed to you by flesh and blood, but by my Father in heaven. And I tell you that you are Peter, and on this rock I will build my church ..." (NIV)

- Confusion about what was ahead for Jesus.

  Matthew 16:22-23 // Peter took him aside and began to rebuke him. "Never, Lord!" he said. "This shall never happen to you!"

  Jesus turned and said to Peter, "Get behind me, Satan! You are a stumbling block to me. You do not have in mind the concerns of God, but merely human concerns." (NIV)

II. A DISTURBING PREDICTION

A. The triple denial.

- Luke 22:31-34 // "Simon, Simon, Satan has asked to sift all of you as wheat. But I have prayed for you, Simon, that your faith may not fail. And when you have turned back, strengthen your brothers."

  But he replied, "Lord, I am ready to go with you to prison and to death."

  Jesus answered, "I tell you, Peter, before the rooster crows today, you will deny three times that you know me." (NIV)

B. Jesus addresses Peter by his given name, Simon, three times.

- We need to remember who we were and who we are and not take it for granted.

- Men and women who follow Jesus can behave badly like Simon the Fisherman or stand firm like Peter the Rock.

C. Peter was sincere and passionate: "I've got this!"

- Peter was about to learn an uncomfortable truth about himself.

- Romans 7:15 // I do not understand what I do. For what I want to do, I do not do, but what I hate, I do. (NIV)

III. PETER'S PAINFUL REALITY

A. When Jesus was arrested, Peter followed at a distance.

B. Peter tried to blend in around a fire.

- Luke 22:56-57 // A servant girl saw him seated there in the firelight. She looked closely at him and said, "This man was with him." But he denied it. "Woman, I don't know him," he said. (NIV)

- Peter changed his position around the fire, and a little later, someone else recognizes him, but Peter adamantly denies it.

- About an hour later, someone else assertively calls him out. Peter curses and swears to them that he absolutely does not know Jesus.

- The rooster crows.

- Luke 22:61-62 // The Lord turned and looked straight at Peter. Then Peter remembered the word the Lord had spoken to him: "Before the rooster crows today, you will disown me three times." And he went outside and wept bitterly. (NIV)

C. After the resurrection of Jesus.

- God's compassion for Peter is highlighted in Mark's account when one of the angels in the tomb told the women with Mary that Jesus had risen and specifically instructed them to go tell the disciples *and* Peter.

- Jesus appeared to the disciples while they were inside a locked room on two different occasions, but He had yet to talk with Peter about his denial.

- Peter announced to his friends that he was going fishing. They fished all night and caught nothing. As the sun was coming up, Jesus stood on the shore.

- John 21:6 // He said, "Throw your net on the right side of the boat, and you will find some." When they did, they were unable to haul the net in because of the large number of fish. (NIV)

IV. A GRACEFUL CONVERSATION

John 21:15-19

Jesus said to Simon Peter, "Simon, son of John,
do you love me more than these?"

He said to him, "Yes, Lord. You know that I love you."

He said to him, "Feed my lambs."
He said to him a second time, "Simon, son of John, do you love me?"

He said to him, "Yes, Lord. You know that I love you."

He said to him, "Tend my sheep."
He said to him the third time, "Simon, son of John, do you love me?"

Peter was grieved because he said to him the third time, "Do you love me?"
And he said to him, "Lord, you know everything. You know that I love you."

Jesus said to him, "Feed my sheep ...
And after saying this, he said to him, "Follow me."

A. A Lesson on **Identity**

- Jesus addressed Peter as Simon, son of John, as He did when He predicted his denial. It was a clarifying moment for him to remember who he was before following Jesus and who he was called to be.

- We need to take our faith off of auto-pilot and reaffirm our identity in Christ daily.

B. A Lesson on **Humility**

- This lesson on humility stuck with Peter and was reflected in his first letter.

- 1 Peter 5:5-6 // … Clothe yourselves with humility toward one another because God opposes the proud but shows favor to the humble. (NIV)

- Peter did not over-correct to passivity. He understood the reality of spiritual warfare and knew how to stand firm in the faith.

- 1 Peter 5:8-9 // Be alert and of sober mind. Your enemy, the devil, prowls around like a roaring lion, looking for someone to devour. Resist him, standing firm in the faith, because you know that the family of believers throughout the world is undergoing the same kind of sufferings. (NIV)

C. A Lesson on **Compassion**

- Jesus never mentioned the details of Peter's denial.

- Jesus modeled the truth of Romans 5:8

- Romans 5:8 // God demonstrates his own love for us in this: While we were still sinners, Christ died for us. (NIV)

D. A Lesson on **Grace**

- Romans 5:20 // Where sin increased, grace increased all the more. (NIV)

- Peter denied Jesus three times, and Jesus asked him three times if he loved Him. Three times, Peter affirmed his love for Jesus, and three times, Jesus confirmed Peter's mission to care for His sheep.

E. A Lesson on **Strength from Failure**

- When Jesus predicted Peter's denial, He said He had prayed for him that when he turned back, he would strengthen others.

- 1 Peter 5:10 // And the God of all grace, who called you to his eternal glory in Christ, after you have suffered a little while, will himself restore you and make you strong, firm, and steadfast. (NIV)

F. A Lesson on **Total Surrender**

- John 21:17 // Peter was hurt because Jesus asked him the third time, "Do you love me?" He said, "Lord, you know all things. You know that I love you." (NIV)

- There was no swagger, posing, or blowing smoke.

- Peter humbly surrendered to the all-knowing God.

V. FINAL THOUGHTS

A. Different responses to the all-knowing God in this series:

- The Israelites in the wilderness thought they knew more than God.

- King Saul was guilty of selective obedience, a clear indicator that he thought he knew better than God.

- King David was self-deceived when a look turned into lust, then lust became adultery, and adultery led to murder. In the moment, he either thought God was unaware, or didn't care.

- David finally repented and surrendered to the all-knowing God he loved.

- Elijah discovered in a gentle whisper that God was with him and knew him not only in the shock-and-awe showdown on Mount Carmel but also in the cave when he was physically, emotionally, and spiritually depleted.

- God warned Israel that He knew what was in their heart and how they had replaced Him with worthless idols. The all-knowing God exposes the deeper idols underneath it all when good people behave badly.

- On the road to Damascus, Saul came face to face with the Lord, who knows everything.

- In the conversation on the beach, Peter humbly surrenders to the all-knowing God.

B. There is nowhere we can go where God isn't. Nothing we can do or say that He doesn't see and hear. And there is nothing in our hearts and minds that He is not fully aware of.

- Luke 12:2-3 // There is nothing concealed that will not be disclosed or hidden that will not be made known. What you have said in the dark will be heard in the daylight, and what you have whispered in the ear in the inner rooms will be proclaimed from the roofs.

The right response to wrong behavior is not to spin it or try and cover it up. The solution is not behavior modification but transformation, asking God to change us from the inside out.

It starts when we humble ourselves in total surrender, as Simon Peter did on the beach when he said:

Lord, you know all things.

You know that I love you.

TALK ABOUT IT

1. When Jesus was arrested, Peter followed at a distance. Have there been times in your life when you have followed Jesus at a safe distance? Explain.

2. Have you ever done something you thought was too big for God to forgive? How did you come to apply God's grace to your sin? (Share the details ONLY if you are in a group of trustworthy friends.)

3. Which of the six lessons in this session from the cautionary tale of Simon Peter encourages you the most? (Identity, Humility, Compassion, Grace, Strength From Failure, Total Surrender)

4. What do you think about the fact that Jesus never mentioned the details of Peter's denial in the conversation on the beach?

5. How does the fact that God knows everything we think and do, yet He still loves us, make you feel? Do you feel guilty, paranoid, or humbled?

6. How does understanding God's grace inspire us to live a life of total surrender?

NOTES

NOTES

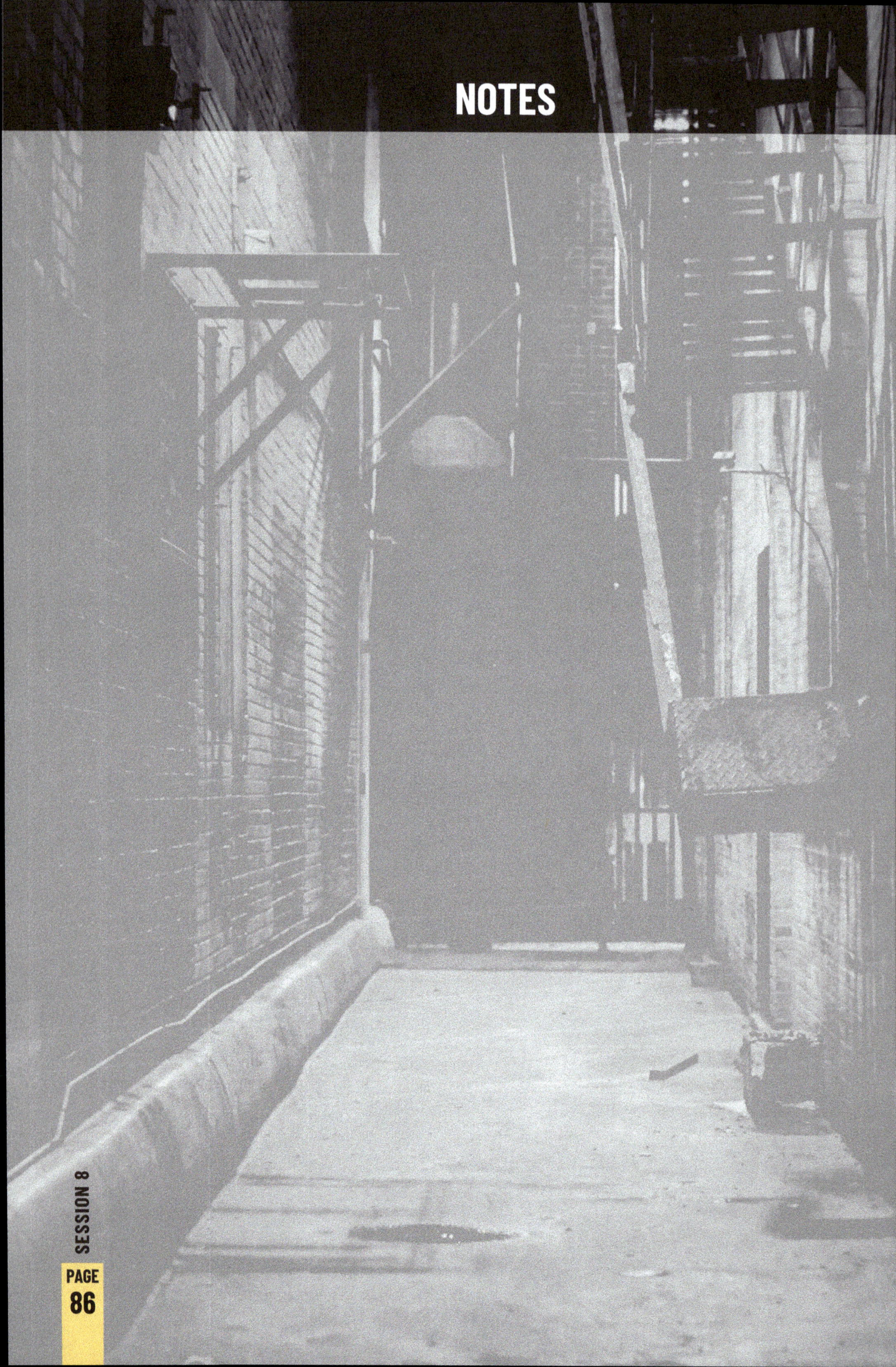

PERSONAL APPLICATION

Information without application leads to frustration. Use this page to write down a few practical and personal steps to help you apply the principles from this series.

The goal is transformation, not behavior modification. The practice of writing down a plan with goals and steps will put you in a better position to experience God's purpose and the life Jesus promised.

Share your plan with a trustworthy friend who will support and pray for you.

GOOD FEED
MEDIA

Free App. Free Content.

Download on the **App Store**

GET IT ON **Google Play**

Quality content for personal growth
and small group discipleship.

GOODFEEDMEDIA.COM

Good People Behaving Badly video teaching sessions are on
the Media Series Channel in the Good Feed Media App.

www.ingramcontent.com/pod-product-compliance
Lightning Source LLC
Chambersburg PA
CBHW081140090426

42736CB00018B/3425